Easy Coleslaw Cookbook

50 Delicious Coleslaw Recipes

By
BookSumo Press
All rights reserved

Published by
http://www.booksumo.com

Table of Contents

Oriental Coleslaw 5

Garden Party Coleslaw 6

Sunflower Coleslaw 7

Famous New England Coleslaw 8

Cookout Coleslaw 9

Colorful Coleslaw 10

November's Coleslaw 11

Restaurant Style Coleslaw 12

Granny Smith Coleslaw 13

Carolinas Style 14

Saint Francis Coleslaw 15

Friday's Bell Pepper Coleslaw 16

Salt Belt Coleslaw 17

Tuesday's Coleslaw Festival 18

Snow Belt Coleslaw 19

Zesty Coleslaw 20

Milanese Coleslaw 21

Bonnie's Coleslaw 22

Sunday Monterey Jack Coleslaw 23

I ♥ Coleslaw 24

Creamy Mustard Dressing for Coleslaws 25

Sleepy Bee Coleslaw 26

Chiang Mai Coleslaw 27

July's Coleslaw 28

Wednesday's Mediterranean Coleslaw 29

Traditional Hawaiian Coleslaw 30

6 Ingredient Coleslaw 31

Quadratic Coleslaw 32

8 Bit Adder Coleslaw 33

Dijon Raisin Coleslaw 34

Mexican Style Coleslaw 35

Crossroads Coleslaw 36

San Antonio Coleslaw 37

Winter's Coleslaw 38

New-Age Coleslaw 39

Classical Coleslaw 40

Pre-Colonial Coleslaw 41

Garden Fresh Coleslaw 42

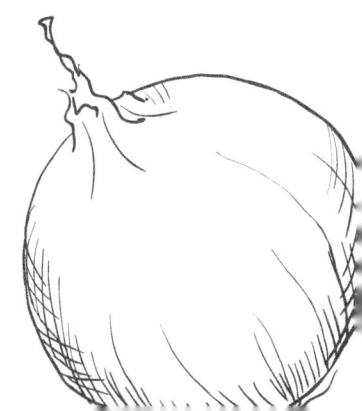

Copycat Chipotle Coleslaw 43

Baltimore Style Coleslaw 44

Hot Cross Coleslaw 45

Thousand Island Coleslaw 46

Manila Coleslaw 47

Catering Coleslaw 48

Bavarian Style Coleslaw 49

Picnic Coleslaw 50

Alabama Inspired Coleslaw 51

Rice Vinegar and Lime Coleslaw 52

Bethany Beach Coleslaw 53

Oriental Coleslaw

Prep Time: 15 mins
Total Time: 25 mins

Servings per Recipe: 4
Calories	253 kcal
Fat	12.5 g
Carbohydrates	30.5g
Protein	7.1 g
Cholesterol	0 mg
Sodium	543 mg

Ingredients

- 2 tbsp vegetable oil
- 3 tbsp white vinegar
- 2 tbsp white sugar
- 1 (3 oz.) package chicken flavored ramen noodles, crushed, seasoning packet reserved
- 1/2 tsp salt
- 1/2 tsp ground black pepper
- 2 tbsp sesame seeds
- 1/4 C. sliced almonds
- 1/2 medium head cabbage, shredded
- 5 green onions, chopped

Directions

1. Set your oven to 350 degrees F before doing anything else.
2. For dressing in a medium bowl, add the oil, vinegar, sugar, ramen noodle spice mix, salt and pepper and beat till well combined.
3. In a medium baking sheet, place the sesame seeds and almonds in a single layer.
4. Cook in the oven for about 10 minutes.
5. In a large salad bowl, mix together the cabbage, green onions and crushed ramen noodles.
6. Add the dressing and toss to coat well.
7. Serve with a topping of the toasted sesame seeds and almonds.

GARDEN PARTY
Coleslaw

🥣 Prep Time: 10 mins
🕐 Total Time: 10 mins

Servings per Recipe: 10
Calories   184 kcal
Fat   12.6 g
Carbohydrates   16.1g
Protein   4 g
Cholesterol   0 mg
Sodium   514 mg

Ingredients

6 tbsp apple cider vinegar
6 tbsp vegetable oil
5 tbsp creamy peanut butter
3 tbsp soy sauce
3 tbsp brown sugar
2 tbsp minced fresh ginger root
1 1/2 tbsp minced garlic
5 C. thinly sliced green cabbage

2 C. thinly sliced red cabbage
2 C. shredded Napa cabbage
2 red bell peppers, thinly sliced
2 carrots, julienned
6 green onions, chopped
1/2 C. chopped fresh cilantro

Directions

1. In a medium bowl, add the rice vinegar, oil, peanut butter, soy sauce, brown sugar, ginger and garlic and beat till well combined.
2. In a large bowl, mix together the green cabbage, red cabbage, Napa cabbage, red bell peppers, carrots, green onions and cilantro.
3. Add the peanut butter mixture and toss to coat just before serving.

Sunflower Coleslaw

Prep Time: 15 mins
Total Time: 1 hr 15 mins

Servings per Recipe: 7
Calories	413 kcal
Fat	31.3 g
Carbohydrates	31.8g
Protein	4.6 g
Cholesterol	0 mg
Sodium	169 mg

Ingredients

- 1 C. olive oil
- 1/3 C. distilled white vinegar
- 1/2 C. white sugar
- 1 (3 oz.) package chicken flavored ramen noodles, crushed, seasoning packet reserved
- 1 large head fresh broccoli, diced
- 2 carrots, grated
- 2 bunches green onions, chopped
- 1 C. sunflower seeds

Directions

1. In a small bowl mix together the oil, vinegar, sugar and the seasoning packet from the ramen noodles and refrigerate for at least 1 hour before serving or overnight.
2. In a large bowl mix together the broccoli, carrots, green onions and sunflower seeds.
3. Crush the ramen noodles and stir in the salad mixture.
4. Place the dressing over salad and keep aside for about 10 minutes before serving.

FAMOUS
New England Coleslaw

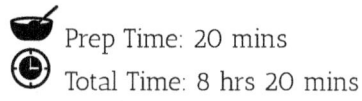

Prep Time: 20 mins
Total Time: 8 hrs 20 mins

Servings per Recipe: 12
Calories 215 kcal
Fat 15.2 g
Carbohydrates 18.7g
Protein 3.2 g
Cholesterol 9 mg
Sodium 462 mg

Ingredients

1 head cabbage, cored and coarsely chopped
1 carrot, grated
1 sweet onion, minced
3 green onions, minced
1 dill pickle, minced
1 C. mayonnaise
2 C. buttermilk
2 tbsp dill pickle juice
2 tbsp vinegar
2 tbsp prepared yellow mustard
1/2 C. white sugar
1 pinch cayenne pepper
1 tsp salt, divided
1 clove garlic

Directions

1. In a large bowl, mix together the cabbage, carrot, sweet onion, green onions and dill pickle.
2. In another bowl, add the mayonnaise, buttermilk, dill pickle juice, vinegar, mustard, sugar, cayenne pepper and 3/4 tsp of the salt.
3. In a small bowl, add the remaining salt and garlic and mash well.
4. Add the mashed garlic into the dressing and beat well.
5. Place the dressing over the slaw and toss to coat.
6. Refrigerate, covered for about 8 hours or overnight before serving.

Cookout Coleslaw

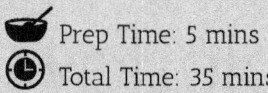

Prep Time: 5 mins
Total Time: 35 mins

Servings per Recipe: 10
Calories   214 kcal
Fat   18.7 g
Carbohydrates   11.4g
Protein   0.8 g
Cholesterol   12 mg
Sodium   174 mg

Ingredients

1 (16 oz.) bag coleslaw mix
1 C. mayonnaise
1/4 C. white sugar
2 tbsp cider vinegar
1/2 tsp onion powder
salt and ground black pepper to taste

Directions

1. In a large bowl, place the coleslaw mix.
2. In a small bowl, add the mayonnaise, sugar, vinegar, onion powder, salt and pepper in a small bowl.
3. Place the mayonnaise mixture over coleslaw mix and toss to coat.
4. Refrigerate for at least 30 minutes.
5. Serve with a slotted spoon.

COLORFUL
Coleslaw

Prep Time: 20 mins
Total Time: 3 hrs 20 mins

Servings per Recipe: 8
Calories   257 kcal
Fat   15.8 g
Carbohydrates   29.9 g
Protein   3.2 g
Cholesterol   5 mg
Sodium   140 mg

Ingredients

1/2 C. almonds
5 C. shredded cabbage
1 1/2 C. dried cranberries
3/4 C. celery, diced
3/4 C. chopped green onion
3/4 C. chopped red bell pepper
Dressing:
1/2 C. mayonnaise (such as Hellman's(R))

1 1/2 tbsp honey mustard
1 1/2 tbsp honey
3 pinches dried basil
salt and ground black pepper to taste

Directions

1. Set your oven to 350 degrees F before doing anything else.
2. Spread the almonds onto a baking sheet.
3. Cook in the oven for about 10 minutes.
4. Remove from the oven and keep aside to cool completely.
5. In a large bowl, mix together the cabbage, cranberries, celery, green onion, red bell pepper and toasted almonds.
6. In a small bowl, add the mayonnaise, honey mustard, honey, basil, salt and pepper and beat till thick and creamy.
7. Place the dressing over the cabbage mixture and stir to coat.
8. With a plastic wrap, cover the bowl and refrigerate for about 3 hours.

November's
Coleslaw

Prep Time: 30 mins
Total Time: 1 hr

Servings per Recipe: 10
Calories   102 kcal
Fat   4.5 g
Carbohydrates   16g
Protein   0.9 g
Cholesterol   2 mg
Sodium   < 37 mg

Ingredients

1 C. halved cranberries
1/4 C. white sugar
2 oranges, peeled and thinly sliced
1 red onion, thinly sliced

4 C. shredded cabbage
1 large apple - peeled, cored, and chopped
1/4 C. mayonnaise

Directions

1. In a small bowl, add the cranberries and sugar and toss to coat.
2. Cover and refrigerate.
3. In a large bowl, mix together the oranges, onion, cabbage, apple and mayonnaise.
4. Add the cranberry mixture and toss to coat just before serving.

RESTAURANT STYLE
Coleslaw

Prep Time: 20 mins
Total Time: 20 mins

Servings per Recipe: 12
Calories	260 kcal
Fat	19.5 g
Carbohydrates	21.1g
Protein	3.6 g
Cholesterol	11 mg
Sodium	186 mg

Ingredients

- 1 1/4 C. mayonnaise
- 1/4 C. sour cream
- 1/4 C. white sugar
- 2 tbsp white balsamic vinegar
- 1 tbsp orange juice
- 1/4 tsp ground black pepper
- 2 1/2 heads cabbage, shredded
- 2 carrots, shredded

Directions

1. In a bowl, add the mayonnaise, sour cream, sugar, white balsamic vinegar, orange juice and pepper and stir to combine well.
2. In a large bowl, mix together the cabbage and carrots.
3. Place the dressing over the cabbage mixture and toss to coat.

Granny Smith Coleslaw

Prep Time: 15 mins
Total Time: 8 hrs 15 mins

Servings per Recipe: 6
Calories	99 kcal
Fat	3.8 g
Carbohydrates	17.1g
Protein	1.1 g
Cholesterol	2 mg
Sodium	< 118 mg

Ingredients

- 4 C. shredded cabbage
- 1 C. shredded carrot
- 1 Granny Smith apple - peeled, cored and coarsely shredded
- 2 tbsp honey
- 1 tbsp brown sugar
- 2 tsp white vinegar
- 1 tbsp pineapple juice (optional)
- 2 tbsp mayonnaise
- 1 dash salt
- 1 tsp ground black pepper

Directions

1. In a bowl, mix together the shredded cabbage, carrot and sliced apple.
2. In another bowl, add the honey, brown sugar, vinegar, pineapple juice and mayonnaise and beat till the honey and sugar is dissolved completely.
3. Place the dressing over the salad and toss to coat.
4. Season with the salt and pepper and toss again.
5. Refrigerate, covered to chill before serving.

CAROLINAS
Style

Prep Time: 20 mins
Total Time: 1 hr 20 mins

Servings per Recipe: 6
Calories   322 kcal
Fat   23.7 g
Carbohydrates   13.4g
Protein   15.4 g
Cholesterol   107 mg
Sodium   879 mg

Ingredients

1 tbsp balsamic vinegar
1 tsp white sugar
1/3 C. mayonnaise
1 tbsp coarse-grain brown mustard
1 head cabbage, cored and shredded
2 hard-cooked eggs, peeled and chopped
6 slices crisply cooked turkey bacon, crumbled
salt and pepper to taste

Directions

1. In a large bowl, mix together the vinegar, sugar, mayonnaise and mustard.
2. Add the cabbage, eggs and bacon and toss lightly to coat with the dressing.
3. Season with the salt and pepper.
4. Refrigerate for about 1 hour before serving.

Saint Francis Coleslaw

Prep Time: 20 mins
Total Time: 20 mins

Servings per Recipe: 6
Calories   143 kcal
Fat   10.8 g
Carbohydrates   10.6 g
Protein   0.9 g
Cholesterol   13 mg
Sodium   356 mg

Ingredients

4 C. shredded cabbage
1 C. shredded carrots
1/3 C. chopped green bell pepper
1/3 C. chopped green onions

1 C. creamy salad dressing
salt and pepper, to taste

Directions

1. In a large bowl, mix together the cabbage, carrots, bell pepper, green onion, salad dressing, salt and pepper.
2. Refrigerate before serving.

FRIDAY'S
Bell Pepper Coleslaw

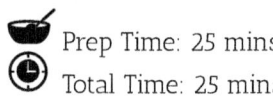
Prep Time: 25 mins
Total Time: 25 mins

Servings per Recipe: 8
Calories	228 kcal
Fat	22 g
Carbohydrates	7.6g
Protein	1.3 g
Cholesterol	10 mg
Sodium	278 mg

Ingredients

- 1 tbsp distilled white vinegar
- 1 C. mayonnaise
- 2 tbsp prepared Dijon-style mustard
- 3 C. shredded cabbage
- 3 C. shredded red cabbage
- 1 C. grated carrot
- 1/2 C. shredded green bell pepper
- 1/2 C. shredded red bell pepper
- 1/2 C. shredded celery

Directions

1. In a small bowl, mix together the vinegar, mayonnaise and mustard.
2. In a large bowl, mix together the cabbage, carrots, bell peppers and celery.
3. Pour dressing over vegetables, mixing to coat evenly.
4. Refrigerate to chill.
5. Serve over the bed of the lettuce leaves.

Salt Belt Coleslaw

Prep Time: 10 mins
Total Time: 10 mins

Servings per Recipe: 8
Calories	233 kcal
Fat	18.4 g
Carbohydrates	16.4g
Protein	0.9 g
Cholesterol	17 mg
Sodium	291 mg

Ingredients

- 1/2 C. mayonnaise
- 3/4 C. creamy salad dressing (e.g. Miracle Whip)
- 2 tbsp prepared horseradish
- 1 1/2 tsp white vinegar
- 1 1/2 tsp dill weed
- 3 1/2 tbsp sugar
- 1 (16 oz.) package coleslaw mix

Directions

1. In a large bowl, add the mayonnaise, creamy salad dressing, horseradish, vinegar, dill weed and sugar and mix till well combined.
2. Add the coleslaw mix and stir to coat.
3. Refrigerate for at least 3 hours before serving.

TUESDAY'S
Coleslaw Festival

 Prep Time: 40 mins
Total Time: 1 hr 50 mins

Servings per Recipe: 8
Calories   249 kcal
Fat   4.4 g
Carbohydrates   46.6 g
Protein   6.6 g
Cholesterol   2 mg
Sodium   < 161 mg

Ingredients

2 1/2 C. elbow macaroni
1 medium red or green bell pepper, chopped
1 medium onion, diced
2 carrots, peeled and finely chopped
1 C. pineapple chunks, drained, 2 tbsp of juice reserved
3 C. finely shredded cabbage
1/2 tsp garlic powder
1 tbsp Dijon-style mustard
2 tsp apple cider vinegar
1 tbsp canola oil
1 tsp white pepper
1 tbsp white sugar
1 C. cherry-flavored yogurt
salt and pepper to taste
1/2 C. fresh shredded coconut
8 maraschino cherries for garnish (optional)

Directions

1. In a large pan of lightly salted boiling water, cook the macaroni for about 8-10 minutes.
2. Drain and rinse under cold water, and again drain well.
3. In a large bowl, and the macaroni, bell pepper, onion, carrot, pineapple, reserved pineapple juice, cabbage and garlic powder and toss to coat well.
4. In a small bowl, mix together the Dijon mustard, vinegar, oil, white pepper, sugar, yogurt, salt and pepper.
5. Place the dressing into the macaroni salad and toss to coat well.
6. Refrigerate, covered for about 1 hour to overnight.
7. Just before serving, toss the salad again to mix.
8. Serve with a garnishing of the coconut and maraschino cherries.

Snow Belt Coleslaw

Prep Time: 30 mins
Total Time: 3 hrs 5 mins

Servings per Recipe: 8
Calories   201 kcal
Fat   7.6 g
Carbohydrates   32.5g
Protein   1.6 g
Cholesterol   0 mg
Sodium   2876 mg

Ingredients

- 6 C. shredded green cabbage
- 1 1/2 C. shredded carrot
- 1 C. shredded red cabbage
- 1/2 C. shredded onion
- 1/4 C. kosher salt
- 1 C. cider vinegar
- 1 C. white sugar
- 1 tbsp celery seed
- 1 tbsp dry mustard
- 1/4 C. vegetable oil
- ground black pepper to taste

Directions

1. Set a colander over sink.
2. In the colander, mix together the green cabbage, carrot red cabbage, and onion and sprinkle with the kosher salt.
3. Keep aside for about 30 minutes to drip.
4. In a small pan, heat the cider vinegar, sugar, celery seed, and dry mustard on medium-low heat, stirring till the sugar dissolves.
5. Remove from the heat and keep aside to cool.
6. Squeeze the cabbage mixture completely and transfer into a serving bowl.
7. Add the vinegar mixture, vegetable oil and black pepper and stir to coat well.
8. Refrigerate for about 2 hours before serving.

ZESTY
Coleslaw

🥣 Prep Time: 15 mins
🕐 Total Time: 1 hr 15 mins

Servings per Recipe: 8
Calories   177 kcal
Fat   13.9 g
Carbohydrates   9.5g
Protein   5.6 g
Cholesterol   6 mg
Sodium   270 mg

Ingredients

1 (10 oz.) package frozen peas, thawed
2 C. finely shredded cabbage
1 green onion, thinly sliced
1/4 C. sour cream
1/4 C. mayonnaise
1 tsp prepared mustard
1 tsp white vinegar

1/4 tsp salt
1/4 tsp curry powder
3/4 C. salted peanuts, coarsely chopped

Directions

1. In a large bowl, mix together the peas, cabbage and green onion.
2. In another bowl, mix together the sour cream, mayonnaise, mustard, vinegar, salt and curry powder.
3. Place the sour cream mixture over the cabbage mixture and toss to coat.
4. Refrigerate, covered for at least 1 hour, or overnight.
5. Serve with a sprinkling of the peanuts.

Milanese Coleslaw

Prep Time: 25 mins
Total Time: 55 mins

Servings per Recipe: 20
Calories	56 kcal
Fat	1.8 g
Carbohydrates	6.2g
Protein	1.3 g
Cholesterol	0 mg
Sodium	126 mg

Ingredients

- 1/2 C. apple cider vinegar
- 3 (1.5 fluid oz.) jiggers triple sec
- 1 tsp salt
- 4 C. shredded green cabbage
- 2 C. shredded purple cabbage
- 2 C. thinly sliced fennel bulbs
- 1 sweet yellow onion, thinly sliced
- 1/2 C. pine nuts

Directions

1. In a salad bowl, add the apple cider vinegar, triple sec and salt and beat till the salt dissolves.
2. Add the green cabbage, purple cabbage, and fennel and toss to coat.
3. Refrigerate to chill for at least 30 minutes.
4. Serve with a sprinkling of the pine nuts.

BONNIE'S
Coleslaw

🍲 Prep Time: 15 mins
🕒 Total Time: 15 mins

Servings per Recipe: 12
Calories   286 kcal
Fat   19.3 g
Carbohydrates   25g
Protein   5.3 g
Cholesterol   5 mg
Sodium   94 mg

Ingredients

Salad:
1 (28 oz.) package coleslaw mix
1 (3 oz.) package beef-flavored ramen noodles
1 C. sunflower seed kernels
1/2 C. slivered almonds
1/2 C. chopped green onions
1 (4 oz.) can sliced water chestnuts, drained

Dressing:
1/2 C. canola oil
1/2 C. vinegar
1/2 C. white sugar

Directions

1. In a large bowl, place the coleslaw mix.
2. Break the ramen noodles into small pieces and add into the coleslaw mix with the sunflower seed kernels, almonds, green onions and water chestnuts.
3. In another bowl, add the ramen noodle seasoning, canola oil, vinegar and sugar and beat till the sugar dissolves.
4. Place the dressing over the salad and toss to coat well.

Sunday
Monterey Jack Coleslaw

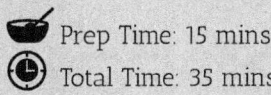 Prep Time: 15 mins
Total Time: 35 mins

Servings per Recipe: 4
Calories	465 kcal
Fat	31.8 g
Carbohydrates	33.5g
Protein	11 g
Cholesterol	66 mg
Sodium	905 mg

Ingredients

- 1 (8 oz.) package three-color (green and red cabbage and carrots) coleslaw blend
- 3/4 C. prepared coleslaw dressing
- 1 C. shredded Cheddar-Monterey Jack cheese blend
- 1/4 tsp salt
- 1/4 tsp ground black pepper
- 2 tbsp butter, softened
- 3/4 C. dry bread crumbs
- 1/4 C. shredded Cheddar-Monterey Jack cheese blend

Directions

1. Set your oven to 400 degrees F before doing anything else.
2. In a bowl, mix coleslaw mix, dressing, 1 C. of the Cheddar-Monterey Jack cheese blend, salt and black pepper.
3. Transfer the coleslaw mixture into a 2-quart baking dish.
4. In another bowl, add the butter, bread crumbs and 1/4 C. of the Cheddar-Monterey Jack cheese blend and mix till well combined.
5. Place the bread crumb mixture over coleslaw mixture evenly.
6. Cook in the oven for about 15-20 minutes.
7. Remove from the oven and keep aside for about 5 minutes before serving.

I
Coleslaw

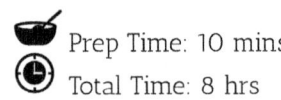 Prep Time: 10 mins
Total Time: 8 hrs

Servings per Recipe: 4
Calories   786 kcal
Fat   55.5 g
Carbohydrates   74.6g
Protein   4.9 g
Cholesterol   0 mg
Sodium   83 mg

Ingredients

1 large head cabbage, shredded
1 green bell pepper, diced
1 onion, finely diced
1 1/2 large carrots, shredded
1 C. white vinegar

1 C. vegetable oil
1 C. white sugar

Directions

1. In a bowl, mix together the cabbage, bell pepper, onion and carrot.
2. In another bowl, add the vinegar, oil and sugar and beat till well combined.
3. Place the dressing over salad and toss to coat.
4. Refrigerate, covered for about 6-8 hours.
5. Drain any excess liquid, toss and serve cold.

Creamy Mustard Dressing for Coleslaws

Prep Time: 10 mins
Total Time: 15 mins

Servings per Recipe: 6
Calories   95 kcal
Fat   7 g
Carbohydrates   7.4g
Protein   1.2 g
Cholesterol   52 mg
Sodium   66 mg

Ingredients

1 egg yolk
3 tbsp white sugar
1 tbsp prepared mustard
2 tbsp butter
1/2 C. white vinegar
1/2 C. half-and-half

Directions

1. In a medium pan, mix together the egg yolk, sugar, mustard, butter and vinegar on medium heat.
2. Boil, beating continuously till the mixture becomes thick.
3. Remove from the heat and keep aside to cool.
4. Add the half-and-half and beat till well combined.
5. Refrigerate before using.

SLEEPY BEE
Coleslaw

🥣 Prep Time: 15 mins
🕐 Total Time: 15 mins

Servings per Recipe: 8
Calories 525 kcal
Fat 46 g
Carbohydrates 29.6g
Protein 2.4 g
Cholesterol 25 mg
Sodium 384 mg

Ingredients

2 C. mayonnaise
1/2 C. honey
1 (16 oz.) package shredded coleslaw mix
4 tbsp celery seed

1 bunch green onions, chopped
salt and pepper to taste

Directions

1. In a large bowl, add the mayonnaise and honey and beat well.
2. Add the coleslaw mix, celery seed, green onions, salt and pepper and mix well.
3. Refrigerator to chill before serving.

Chiang Mai Coleslaw

Prep Time: 20 mins
Total Time: 20 mins

Servings per Recipe: 12
Calories   313 kcal
Fat   25.1 g
Carbohydrates   18.3g
Protein   7.7 g
Cholesterol   15 mg
Sodium   279 mg

Ingredients

1 head cabbage, cored and shredded
2 bunches green onions, chopped
1 (16 oz.) package frozen green peas
1 C. dry roasted peanuts
1 C. sour cream
1 C. mayonnaise
1/4 C. white vinegar

2 tbsp curry powder
1/2 tsp ground ginger
1 tsp ground cayenne pepper

Directions

1. In a large bowl, mix together the cabbage, green onions, peas and peanuts.
2. In another bowl, add the sour cream, mayonnaise, vinegar, curry powder, ginger and cayenne pepper and mix till smooth.
3. Place the dressing over the slaw and toss to coat.
4. Refrigerate, covered before serving.

WEDNESDAY'S
Coleslaw

Prep Time: 15 mins
Total Time: 2 hrs 15 mins

Servings per Recipe: 12
Calories 786 kcal
Fat 55.5 g
Carbohydrates 74.6 g
Protein 4.9 g
Cholesterol 0 mg
Sodium 23 mg

Ingredients

1/4 C. honey
3 tbsp vegetable oil
3 tbsp apple cider vinegar
1/4 tsp salt
1 tsp ground black pepper
4 C. shredded green cabbage
2 2/3 C. shredded red cabbage
1/2 C. thinly sliced green onion
2 carrots, peeled and shredded
1 C. minced red bell pepper

Directions

1. In a large bowl, add the honey, vegetable oil, vinegar, salt and pepper and beat well.
2. Add the green, red cabbage, green onion, carrots and red pepper and toss to coat well.
3. Refrigerate, covered for several hours before serving.

Wednesday's Mediterranean Coleslaw

Prep Time: 15 mins
Total Time: 25 mins

Servings per Recipe: 6
Calories 20 kcal
Fat < 0.1 g
Carbohydrates < 4.7g
Protein 0.6 g
Cholesterol 0 mg
Sodium 209 mg

Ingredients

1 serving cooking spray
1 C. shredded cabbage
1 C. shredded red cabbage
1/2 C. shredded carrots
1 tsp garlic powder
1 tsp onion powder
1/2 tsp salt
1/2 tsp black pepper
1/4 C. balsamic vinegar

Directions

1. Grease a large skillet with cooking spray and heat on medium-high heat.
2. Add the cabbage, red cabbage and carrots and cook for about 2 minutes.
3. Stir in the garlic powder, onion powder, salt and pepper and cook for about 8-10 minutes.
4. Stir in the balsamic vinegar and immediately, remove from the heat.

TRADITIONAL Hawaiian Coleslaw

Prep Time: 40 mins
Total Time: 1 hr 40 mins

Servings per Recipe: 8
Calories 80 kcal
Fat 4.4 g
Carbohydrates 8.3g
Protein 3.5 g
Cholesterol 0 mg
Sodium 415 mg

Ingredients

3 tbsp creamy peanut butter
2 cloves garlic, minced
1/2 tsp salt
2 tbsp rice vinegar
2 tbsp soy sauce
1/8 tsp hot pepper sauce (e.g. Tabasco(TM))

1/2 C. chopped cilantro leaves
2 tbsp chopped fresh chives
2 red bell peppers, thinly sliced
8 C. shredded cabbage
2 tbsp toasted sesame seeds (optional)

Directions

1. In a large bowl, add the peanut butter, garlic, salt, rice vinegar, soy sauce and hot pepper sauce and mix till smooth.
2. Add the cilantro, chives, red pepper and shredded cabbage and mix well. S
3. With a plastic wrap, cover the bowl and refrigerate for about 1 hour.
4. Serve with a sprinkling of the sesame seeds.

6 *Ingredient*
Coleslaw

Prep Time: 10 mins
Total Time: 40 mins

Servings per Recipe: 12
Calories	343 kcal
Fat	31.3 g
Carbohydrates	14.7g
Protein	2 g
Cholesterol	21 mg
Sodium	247 mg

Ingredients

- 2 C. mayonnaise
- 1 C. buttermilk
- 3 tbsp white sugar
- 1 tsp celery seed
- 1/2 tsp ground black pepper
- 2 (16 oz.) packages shredded coleslaw mix

Directions

1. In a large bowl, add the mayonnaise, buttermilk, sugar, celery seed and black pepper and mix well.
2. Fold in the coleslaw mix and refrigerate to chill before serving.

QUADRATIC
Coleslaw

🥣 Prep Time: 15 mins
🕐 Total Time: 1 hr 5 mins

Servings per Recipe: 8
Calories 261 kcal
Fat 22 g
Carbohydrates 16.6g
Protein 2 g
Cholesterol 10 mg
Sodium 474 mg

Ingredients

1 medium head green cabbage, rinsed and very thinly sliced
1 large carrot, shredded
1 (15 oz.) can crushed pineapple, drained
1 C. mayonnaise
1 tsp salt

Directions

1. In a large bowl, mix together the cabbage, carrot, pineapple, mayonnaise and salt.
2. Refrigerate to chill for at least 1 hour before serving.

8 Bit Adder Coleslaw

Prep Time: 10 mins
Total Time: 40 mins

Servings per Recipe: 6
Calories	144 kcal
Fat	9.8 g
Carbohydrates	14.5g
Protein	1.2 g
Cholesterol	5 mg
Sodium	275 mg

Ingredients

- 4 C. shredded cabbage
- 1 (11 oz.) can mandarin oranges, drained and liquid reserved
- 1/2 tsp salt
- 1/4 tsp ground ginger
- 1/4 tsp ground allspice
- 1/4 tsp white pepper
- 1 C. crushed pineapple, drained
- 1/3 C. mayonnaise

Directions

1. In a large bowl, mix together the cabbage, 1 tbsp of the reserved orange juice, salt, ginger, allspice and pepper.
2. Add the oranges and pineapple and toss to coat well.
3. Add the mayonnaise and stir till coated completely.
4. Refrigerate to chill well before serving.

DIJON
Raisin Coleslaw

Prep Time: 15 mins
Total Time: 1 hr 15 mins

Servings per Recipe: 7
Calories   150 kcal
Fat   9.9 g
Carbohydrates 15.3g
Protein   1.7 g
Cholesterol   10 mg
Sodium   175 mg

Ingredients

1 red onion, thinly sliced
1 red bell pepper, thinly sliced
3 C. shredded cabbage
1 large carrot, shredded
1/2 C. raisins

1/4 C. mayonnaise
1/2 C. sour cream
2 tbsp Dijon-style prepared mustard
1 tsp white vinegar

Directions

1. In a large bowl, mix together the onion, red pepper, cabbage, carrot and raisins.
2. In a small bowl, add the mayonnaise, sour cream, mustard and vinegar and beat till well combined.
3. Place the dressing over vegetable mixture and toss to coat well.
4. Refrigerate for at least 2 hours before serving.

Mexican Style
Coleslaw

Prep Time: 10 mins
Total Time: 10 mins

Servings per Recipe: 3
Calories	415 kcal
Fat	40.1 g
Carbohydrates	13.7g
Protein	2 g
Cholesterol	20 mg
Sodium	638 mg

Ingredients

1/2 (16 oz.) package shredded coleslaw mix
1/2 tsp seasoning salt
1 tbsp lemon juice
2 tbsp olive oil
1/2 C. mayonnaise
1/2 C. salsa

Directions

1. In a large bowl, add the coleslaw, seasoning salt, lemon juice, olive oil, mayonnaise and salsa and toss till well combined.
2. Serve immediately.

CROSSROADS
Coleslaw

Prep Time: 30 mins
Total Time: 30 mins

Servings per Recipe: 20
Calories	131 kcal
Fat	8.4 g
Carbohydrates	14.1g
Protein	0.9 g
Cholesterol	0 mg
Sodium	364 mg

Ingredients

- 1 medium head cabbage, shredded
- 1 large red onion, diced
- 1 C. grated carrots
- 2 stalks celery, chopped
- 1 C. white sugar
- 1 C. white vinegar
- 3/4 C. vegetable oil
- 1 tbsp salt
- 1 tbsp dry mustard
- black pepper to taste

Directions

1. In a large bowl, mix together the cabbage, onion, carrots and celery.
2. Sprinkle with 1 C. of the sugar and mix well.
3. In a small pan, mix together the vinegar, oil, salt, dry mustard and pepper and bring to a boil.
4. Place the hot dressing over the cabbage mixture and mix well.

San Antonio Coleslaw

Prep Time: 15 mins
Total Time: 1 hr 15 mins

Servings per Recipe: 8
Calories	236 kcal
Fat	22.2 g
Carbohydrates	9.4g
Protein	2.1 g
Cholesterol	10 mg
Sodium	476 mg

Ingredients

- 1 C. mayonnaise
- 1 tbsp lime juice
- 1 tbsp ground cumin
- 1 tsp cayenne pepper
- 1 tsp salt
- 1 tsp ground black pepper
- 1 medium head green cabbage, rinsed and very thinly sliced
- 1 large carrot, shredded
- 2 green onions, sliced
- 2 radishes, sliced

Directions

1. In a large bowl, add the mayonnaise, lime juice, cumin, salt and pepper and beat till well combined.
2. Add the cabbage, carrot, green onions and radishes and mix till well combined
3. Refrigerate to chill for at least 1 hour before serving.

WINTER'S
Coleslaw

Prep Time: 15 mins
Total Time: 1 hr 15 mins

Servings per Recipe: 8
Calories   184 kcal
Fat   12.6 g
Carbohydrates   17.1g
Protein   1.4 g
Cholesterol   11 mg
Sodium   248 mg

Ingredients

1 (16 oz.) package coleslaw mix
2 tbsp minced onion
1/3 C. white sugar
1/2 tsp salt
1/8 tsp ground black pepper
1/4 C. milk

1/2 C. mayonnaise
1/4 C. buttermilk
1 1/2 tbsp white vinegar
2 1/2 tbsp lemon juice

Directions

1. In a large bowl, mix together the coleslaw and onion.
2. In another bowl, add the sugar, salt, pepper, milk, mayonnaise, buttermilk, vinegar and lemon juice and mix till smooth.
3. Place the dressing over the coleslaw and onion and mix well.
4. Refrigerate to chill for at least 1 hour before serving.

New-Age Coleslaw

Prep Time: 10 mins
Total Time: 1 hr 10 mins

Servings per Recipe: 8
Calories	256 kcal
Fat	23.3 g
Carbohydrates	11.4g
Protein	1.1 g
Cholesterol	15 mg
Sodium	315 mg

Ingredients

- 1 C. mayonnaise
- 2 tbsp sugar
- 1/2 tsp salt
- 1/2 tsp pepper
- 1/2 tsp celery seed
- 1/2 tsp garlic powder
- 1/2 tsp onion powder
- 2 tbsp cider vinegar
- 1 (16 oz.) package shredded coleslaw mix

Directions

1. In a large bowl, add the mayonnaise, sugar, salt, pepper, celery seed, garlic powder, onion powder and cider vinegar and mix well.
2. Add the coleslaw mix and toss to coat.
3. Refrigerate to chill for at least 1 hour before serving.

CLASSICAL
Coleslaw

Prep Time: 15 mins
Total Time: 8 hrs 15 mins

Servings per Recipe: 12
Calories	108 kcal
Fat	7.4 g
Carbohydrates	10.3g
Protein	1.1 g
Cholesterol	4 mg
Sodium	80 mg

Ingredients

1/2 C. mayonnaise
1/3 C. white sugar
1/4 C. milk
2 1/2 tbsp lemon juice
1 1/2 tbsp vinegar
salt and pepper to taste

9 1/2 C. shredded cabbage
1/2 C. grated carrots
1/4 C. minced sweet onion

Directions

1. In a large bowl, add the mayonnaise, sugar, milk, lemon juice, vinegar and salt and pepper and beat till well combined.
2. Add the cabbage, carrots and onion and mix well.
3. Refrigerate for at least 3 hours or up to overnight before serving.

Pre-Colonial
Coleslaw

Prep Time: 15 mins
Total Time: 1 hr 15 mins

Servings per Recipe: 8
Calories	182 kcal
Fat	16.5 g
Carbohydrates	8.2g
Protein	1.8 g
Cholesterol	3 mg
Sodium	434 mg

Ingredients

1 medium head green cabbage, finely shredded
3 tbsp finely chopped garlic
1 1/2 tsp kosher salt
1/3 C. grapeseed oil
1/3 C. mayonnaise
1/3 C. apple cider vinegar
1/4 tsp ground paprika
1/4 tsp ground white pepper
1/8 tsp white sugar
1/8 tsp celery seed

Directions

1. In a large bowl, place the shredded cabbage.
2. Place the chopped garlic into a mound on a cutting board and sprinkle with the salt.
3. With the flat side of a chef's knife, smash the garlic and salt together and transfer into a bowl.
4. Add the grapeseed oil, mayonnaise, apple cider vinegar, ground paprika, ground white pepper, sugar and celery seed in the bowl with the garlic mixture and beat till smooth.
5. Place the dressing over the shredded cabbage and toss to coat well.
6. With the back of a spoon, press the coleslaw down in the bowl and refrigerate, covered for at least 1 hour.
7. Stir well before serving.

GARDEN FRESH
Coleslaw

Prep Time: 15 mins
Total Time: 1 hr 45 mins

Servings per Recipe: 12
Calories	31 kcal
Fat	1.6 g
Carbohydrates	4g
Protein	0.6 g
Cholesterol	2 mg
Sodium	< 126 mg

Ingredients

2 C. shredded zucchini
1 C. shredded carrot
1/4 C. low-fat creamy salad dressing
(such as Miracle Whip Light(R))

1 tsp white sugar
salt and ground black pepper to taste

Directions

1. In a colander, add the zucchini and keep aside for about 30 minutes to drain completely.
2. In a large salad bowl, mix together the zucchini and carrot.
3. Add the creamy salad dressing and sugar and stir to combine.
4. Refrigerate to chill for about 1 hour.
5. Season with the salt and black pepper and stir again.

Copycat Chipotle Coleslaw

Prep Time: 30 mins
Total Time: 30 mins

Servings per Recipe: 8
Calories   41 kcal
Fat   0.3 g
Carbohydrates   < 9.3g
Protein   1.6 g
Cholesterol   0 mg
Sodium   73 mg

Ingredients

4 C. chopped or shredded cabbage
1 medium red bell pepper, chopped
1 C. thinly sliced green onions
1 C. cooked corn kernels
1/2 C. rice vinegar
1/3 C. Splenda no-calorie sweetener
Salt and pepper, to taste (optional)
1 tbsp finely minced jalapeno pepper, seeds and veins removed (optional)
1/2 C. chopped cilantro (optional)

Directions

1. Toss all ingredients together.
2. In a bowl, add all the ingredients and toss to coat well.

BALTIMORE STYLE
Coleslaw

Prep Time: 20 mins
Total Time: 20 mins

Servings per Recipe: 8
Calories	115 kcal
Fat	11 g
Carbohydrates	4.2g
Protein	0.6 g
Cholesterol	5 mg
Sodium	152 mg

Ingredients

1/2 C. mayonnaise
2 tbsp chopped onion
1 tbsp vinegar
2 tsp white sugar
1 tsp seafood seasoning (such as Old Bay(R))

3 C. shredded cabbage
1/2 C. shredded carrots
1/4 C. chopped green bell pepper

Directions

1. In a large salad bowl, add the mayonnaise, onion, vinegar, sugar and seafood seasoning and beat till the sugar is dissolved.
2. Add the cabbage, carrots and green bell pepper and stir to combine well.

Hot Cross Coleslaw

Prep Time: 15 mins
Total Time: 2 hrs 15 mins

Servings per Recipe: 6
Calories   109 kcal
Fat   7.2 g
Carbohydrates   11.1g
Protein   0.9 g
Cholesterol   0 mg
Sodium   125 mg

Ingredients

- 3 tbsp apple cider vinegar
- 3 tbsp canola oil
- 3 tbsp white sugar
- 1/4 tsp dry mustard
- 1/4 tsp poppy seeds
- 1/4 tsp ground black pepper
- 1/4 tsp salt
- 1/4 tsp hot pepper sauce (optional)
- 4 C. shredded green cabbage
- 2 carrots, shredded

Directions

1. In a bowl, add the apple cider vinegar, canola oil, sugar, dry mustard, poppy seeds, black pepper, salt and hot pepper and mix till the sugar is dissolved.
2. In a large salad bowl, mix together the cabbage and carrots.
3. Place the dressing over the slaw and stir to coat.
4. Refrigerate for at least 2 hours before serving.

THOUSAND ISLAND
Coleslaw

Prep Time: 10 mins
Total Time: 10 mins

Servings per Recipe: 6
Calories 27 kcal
Fat 2 g
Carbohydrates 2.5g
Protein < 0.1 g
Cholesterol < 2 mg
Sodium < 242 mg

Ingredients

1 (10 oz.) package angel hair-style shredded cabbage
2 tbsp Thousand Island dressing
2 tbsp seasoned rice vinegar
1 tsp hot sauce
1 pinch salt

Directions

1. In a bowl, add the cabbage, Thousand Island dressing, rice vinegar, hot sauce and with a fork, mix till well combined.

Manila Coleslaw

Prep Time: 15 mins
Total Time: 20 mins

Servings per Recipe: 4
Calories	302 kcal
Fat	22.5 g
Carbohydrates	25.6 g
Protein	2.5 g
Cholesterol	10 mg
Sodium	303 mg

Ingredients

- 1/2 small head green cabbage, cored and thinly sliced
- 1/2 jicama, sliced into matchsticks
- 1 large sweet apple (such as Fuji), sliced into matchsticks
- 1/2 C. mayonnaise
- 1/4 C. pineapple juice
- 1 tsp white sugar
- hot sauce to taste
- salt and freshly ground black pepper to taste
- 1/4 bunch chopped fresh cilantro
- 1/3 oz. toasted corn bits (such as Corn Nuts (R)), crushed

Directions

1. In a large bowl, mix together the cabbage, jicama, and apple.
2. In another bowl, add the mayonnaise, pineapple juice, sugar, hot sauce, salt and pepper and beat till smooth and fluffy.
3. Place the mayonnaise mixture over the cabbage, jicama, and apple and toss to coat.
4. Keep aside for about 5 minutes.
5. Add the cilantro and toss again.
6. Serve immediately with a garnishing of the toasted corn bits.

CATERING
Coleslaw

Prep Time: 15 mins
Total Time: 2 hrs 15 mins

Servings per Recipe: 8
Calories   160 kcal
Fat   11.4 g
Carbohydrates   14.6g
Protein   1.3 g
Cholesterol   6 mg
Sodium   103 mg

Ingredients

1/2 C. mayonnaise
1/3 C. white sugar
1/4 C. milk
2 tbsp lemon juice
1 1/2 tbsp white vinegar
2 tsp sour cream
1/2 tsp freshly ground black pepper
1 pinch cayenne pepper, or to taste

1 lb. cabbage, cut into wedges
2 carrots
1/4 small onion, chopped

Directions

1. In a bowl, add the mayonnaise, sugar, milk, lemon juice, vinegar, sour cream, black pepper and cayenne pepper and mix till well combined.
2. In a food processor, add the cabbage, carrots and onion and with a grater attachment, shred them.
3. Transfer the vegetables mixture in a large bowl.
4. Add the mayonnaise mixture and stir to combine.
5. Refrigerate, covered for at least 2 hours or overnight.
6. Stir coleslaw before serving.

Bavarian Style Coleslaw

Prep Time: 10 mins
Total Time: 2 hrs 10 mins

Servings per Recipe: 6
Calories	183 kcal
Fat	14.7 g
Carbohydrates	12.7g
Protein	1.5 g
Cholesterol	7 mg
Sodium	316 mg

Ingredients

- 1/2 head cabbage, thinly sliced
- 3 tbsp white sugar
- 3 tbsp cider vinegar
- 1/2 tsp celery seed
- 1/2 tsp salt
- 1/2 C. mayonnaise

Directions

1. In a large bowl, place the cabbage.
2. In another bowl, mix together the sugar, vinegar, celery seed and salt.
3. Add the mayonnaise and mix till dressing is smooth and creamy.
4. Place the dressing over the cabbage and toss to coat.
5. Refrigerator for about 2-3 hours.
6. Stir well before serving.

PICNIC
Coleslaw

Prep Time: 10 mins
Total Time: 10 mins

Servings per Recipe: 12
Calories   209 kcal
Fat   16.8 g
Carbohydrates   13.6 g
Protein   1.7 g
Cholesterol   13 mg
Sodium   294 mg

Ingredients

1 (16 oz.) package shredded coleslaw mix
2 C. seedless red grapes, halved
1/2 C. shredded carrot
1 C. mayonnaise
1/4 C. prepared Dijon-style mustard
1/3 C. crumbled blue cheese
2 tbsp white sugar
2 tbsp cider vinegar

Directions

1. In a large bowl, add mayonnaise, mustard, cheese, sugar and vinegar and beat till well combined.
2. Add the coleslaw mix, grapes and carrots and stir till well combined.
3. Refrigerate to chill before serving.

Alabama Inspired Coleslaw

Prep Time: 20 mins
Total Time: 2 hrs 20 mins

Servings per Recipe: 8
Calories	184 kcal
Fat	11.3 g
Carbohydrates	20.3g
Protein	2.7 g
Cholesterol	6 mg
Sodium	274 mg

Ingredients

- 1 head cabbage, finely shredded
- 2 carrots, finely chopped
- 2 tbsp finely chopped onion
- 1/2 C. mayonnaise
- 1/3 C. white sugar
- 1/4 C. milk
- 1/4 C. buttermilk
- 2 tbsp lemon juice
- 2 tbsp distilled white vinegar
- 1/2 tsp salt
- 1/8 tsp ground black pepper

Directions

1. In a large salad bowl, mix together the cabbage, carrots and onion.
2. In another bowl, add the mayonnaise, sugar, milk, buttermilk, lemon juice, vinegar, salt and black pepper and beat till smooth and the sugar is dissolved.
3. Place the dressing over cabbage mixture and mix till well combined.
4. Refrigerate, covered for at least 2 hours.
5. Just before serving, mix again before serving.

RICE VINEGAR and Lime Coleslaw

Prep Time: 25 mins
Total Time: 25 mins

Servings per Recipe: 7
Calories   189 kcal
Fat   18.8 g
Carbohydrates   5.6g
Protein   0.9 g
Cholesterol   9 mg
Sodium   164 mg

Ingredients

3/4 C. mayonnaise
1 lime, zested
2 tsp fresh lime juice
1/2 tsp rice vinegar
2 cloves garlic, minced
2 tsp sweet chili sauce

2 tsp white sugar
3 tbsp finely chopped fresh cilantro
1/4 red onion, finely diced
4 C. shredded green cabbage

Directions

1. In a large bowl, add the mayonnaise, lime zest, lime juice, rice vinegar, garlic, sweet chili sauce and sugar and mix till the sugar dissolves.
2. Add the cilantro and red onion and stir to combine.
3. Slowly, add the cabbage about 1 C. at a time, mixing till all the cabbage is coated.

Bethany Beach Coleslaw

Prep Time: 15 mins
Total Time: 2 hrs 15 mins

Servings per Recipe: 6
Calories   252 kcal
Fat   22.2 g
Carbohydrates   11.2g
Protein   3.6 g
Cholesterol   11 mg
Sodium   185 mg

Ingredients

1 (12 oz.) package tri-color coleslaw mix (with green cabbage, red cabbage and carrots)
3/4 C. halved and thickly sliced celery stalks
2 tbsp chopped white onion
1/3 C. sliced green onions
1/2 C. salted sunflower kernels
1/2 C. mayonnaise
2 tbsp white vinegar
sea salt to taste
1/2 tsp ground black pepper

Directions

1. In a large salad bowl, mix together the coleslaw mix, celery, white and green onion and sunflower kernels.
2. Add the mayonnaise, white vinegar, salt and black pepper and stir to combine.
3. Refrigerate for overnight.

Printed in Great Britain
by Amazon